MW00952908

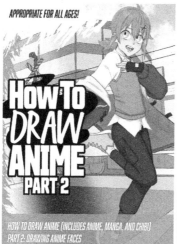

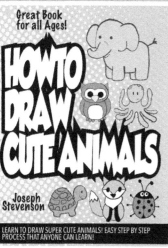

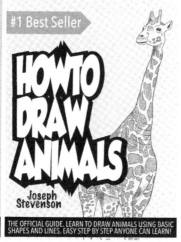

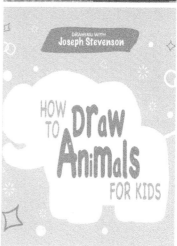

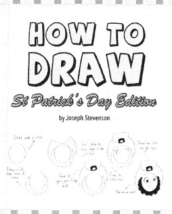

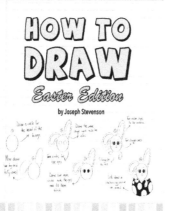

EASTER BUNNY

Draw a circle for the head of the bunny.

①

Now draw two big and fluffy ears!

②

Draw the same shape again inside the ears.

③

Two circles for the eyes.

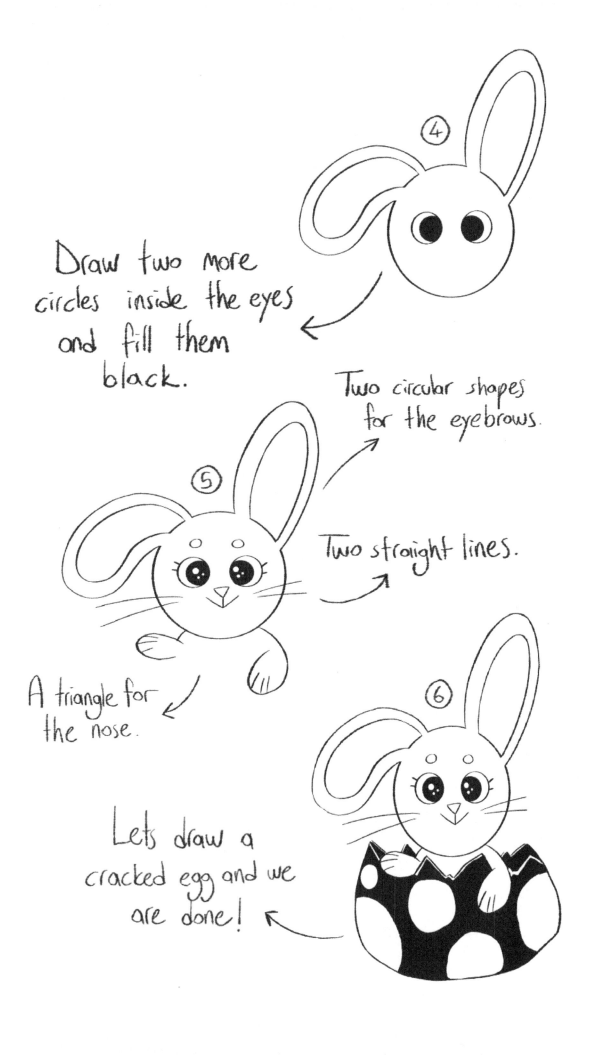

④

Draw two more circles inside the eyes and fill them black.

Two circular shapes for the eyebrows.

⑤

Two straight lines.

A triangle for the nose.

⑥

Lets draw a cracked egg and we are done!

BASKET

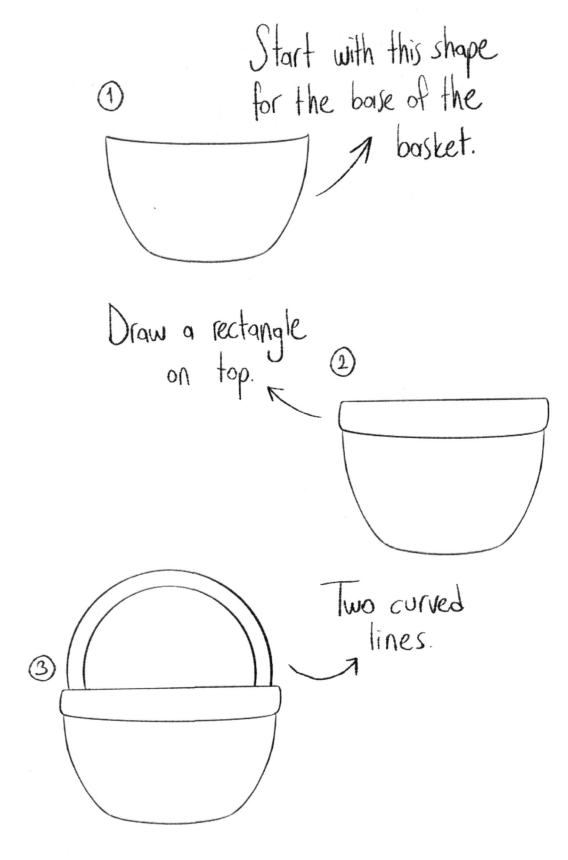

Start with this shape for the base of the basket.

①

Draw a rectangle on top.

②

③

Two curved lines.

Add these lines for the texture. ④

Put some eggs in the basket.

⑤

Complete the drawing with a ribbon.

⑥

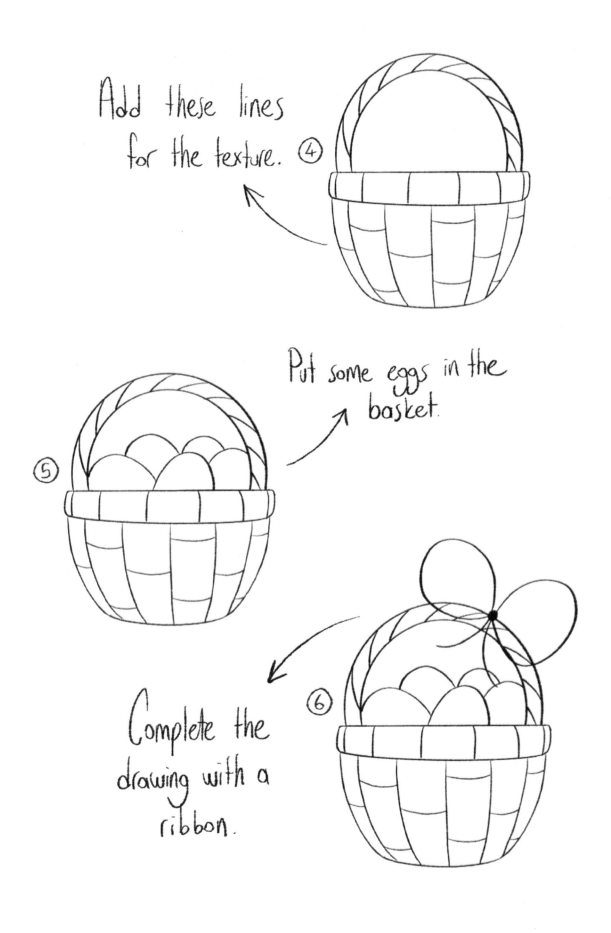

CHICK

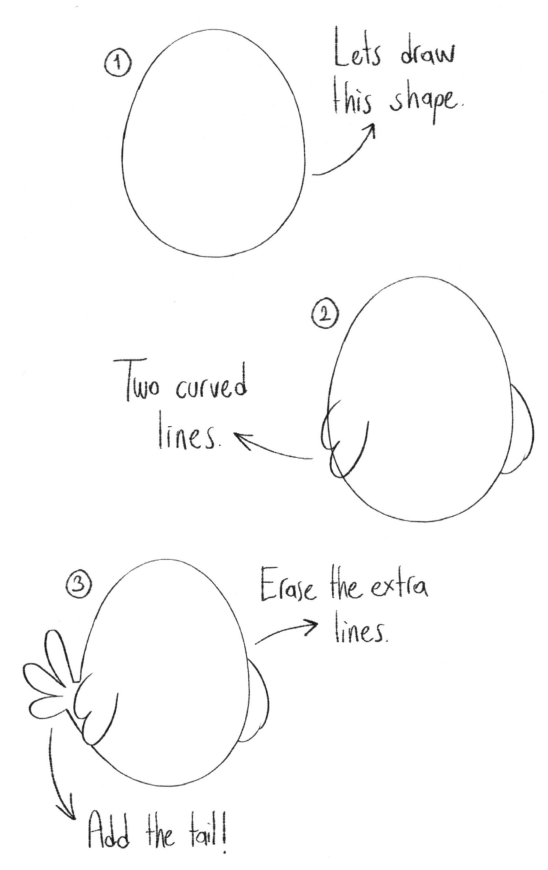

① Lets draw this shape.

② Two curved lines.

③ Erase the extra lines.

Add the tail!

④ A triangle for the beak and two circles for the eyes.

⑤ Don't forget to draw his small feet!

We will complete the drawing with a few easter eggs!

⑥

EASTER EGG

Start with a
circle.

①

Draw a curved
line on top.

②

③

Draw random
circles on top.

Erase the extra
lines.

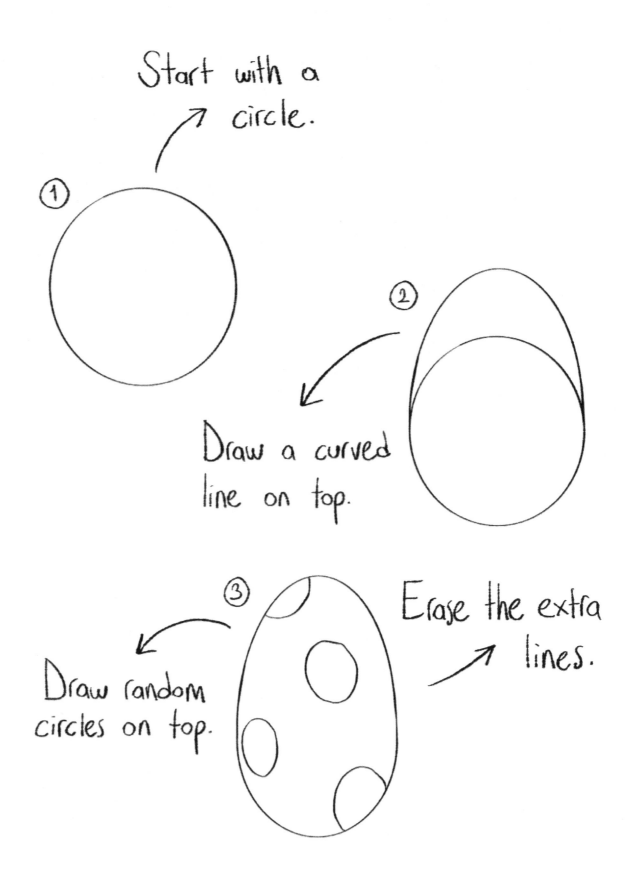

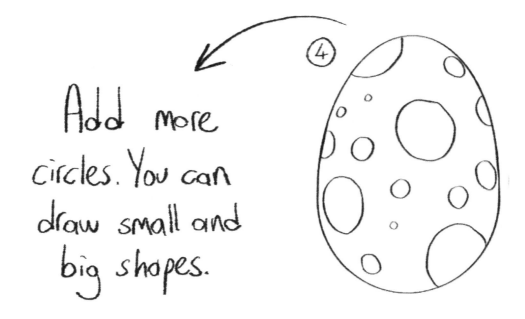

Add more circles. You can draw small and big shapes.

④

⑤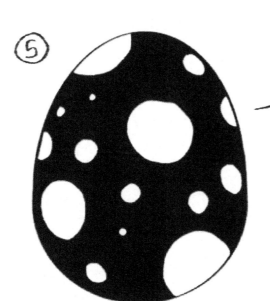

Fill it black.

Draw simple spirals inside each circle.

⑥

TULIP

Draw two lines.

①

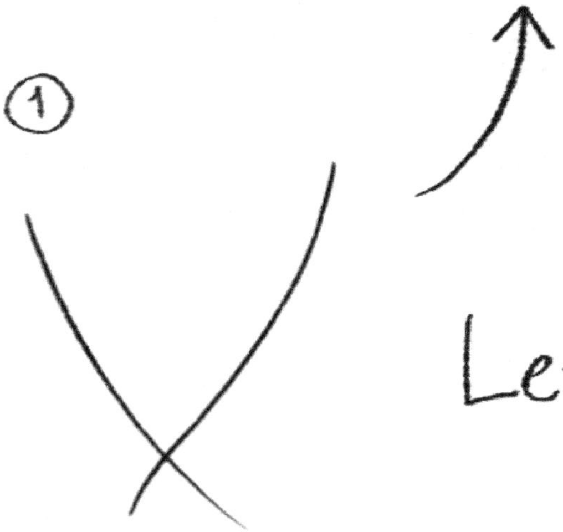

Lets add a few leaves.

②

Lets add two curved lines on top of each line.

③

Lets add
this shape.
④

Draw the
same shape two
more times.
⑤

Add curved lines
inside each shape.
⑥

DAFFODIL

① Start with two lines.

② Draw this basic shape.

③ Lets draw this on top of each line.

④ Draw curved lines inside.

⑤ Think these shapes as triangles.

⑥ Draw curved lines on top and we are done!

BLOSSOM

① Start with a simple shape for the first petal.

② Draw the same shape again.

Keep drawing more petals until it formes a flower.

Erase the extra
lines.

④

Draw random lines
inside each petal.

⑤

⑥

Draw a circle, fill it
black and draw random
lines on it.

BUD

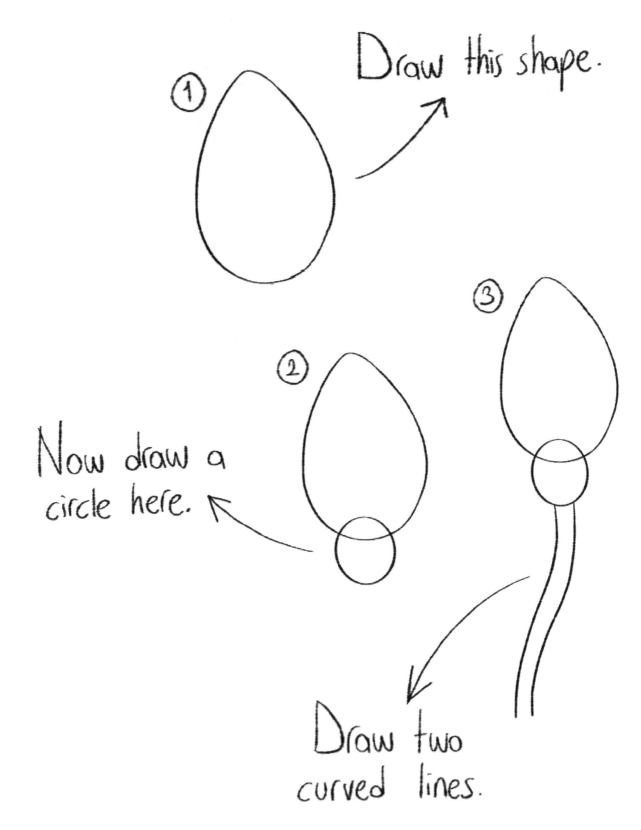

① Draw this shape.

② Now draw a circle here.

③ Draw two curved lines.

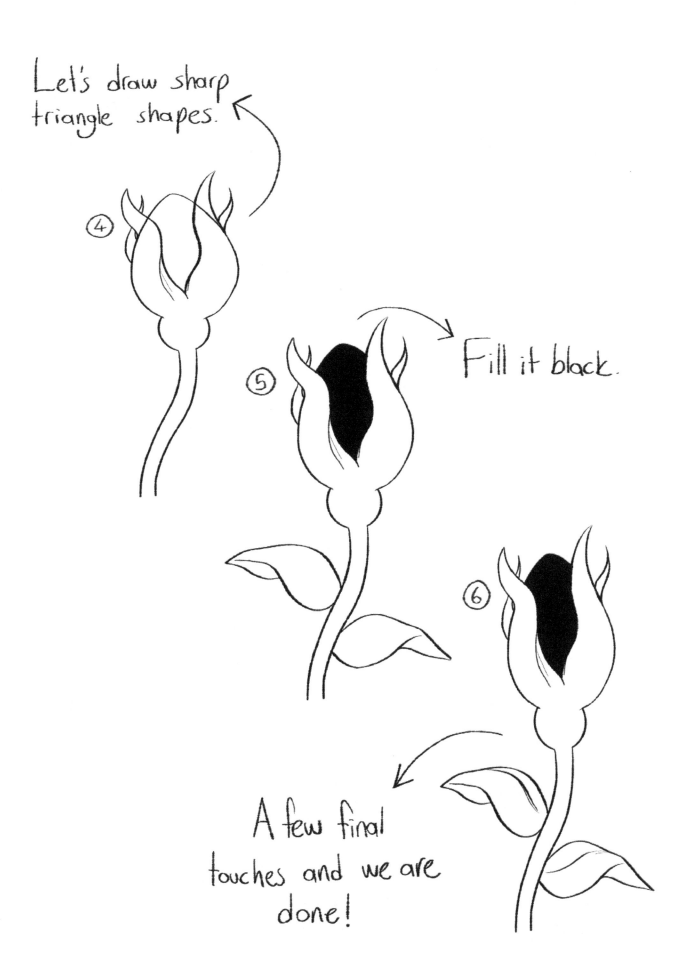

Let's draw sharp
triangle shapes.

④

⑤

Fill it black.

⑥

A few final
touches and we are
done!

SEEDS

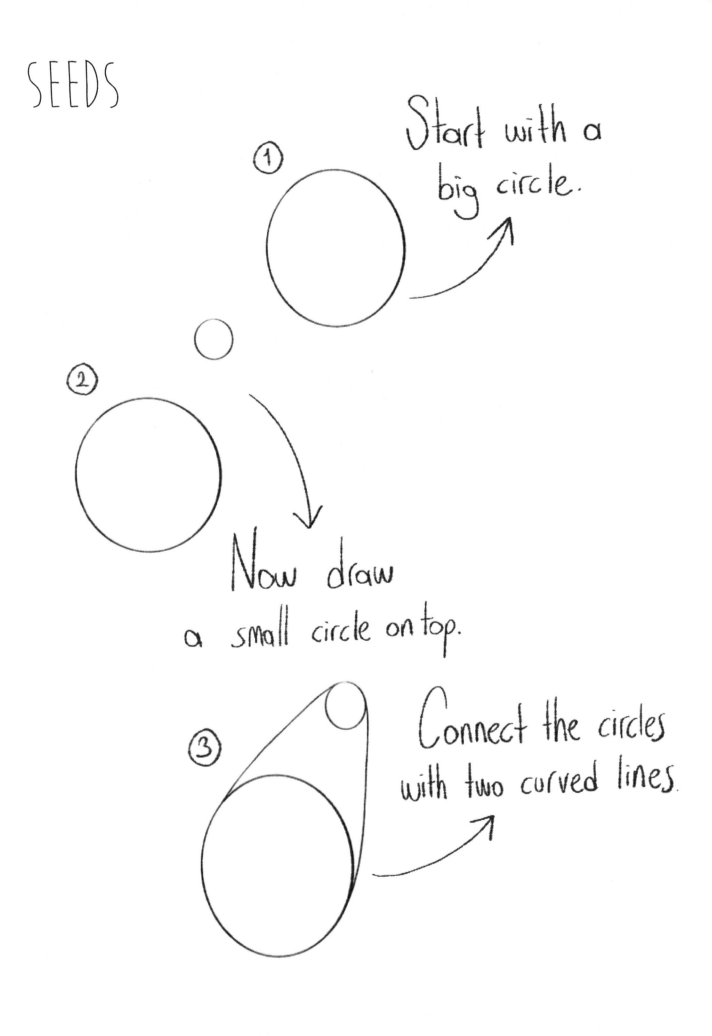

① Start with a big circle.

② Now draw a small circle on top.

③ Connect the circles with two curved lines.

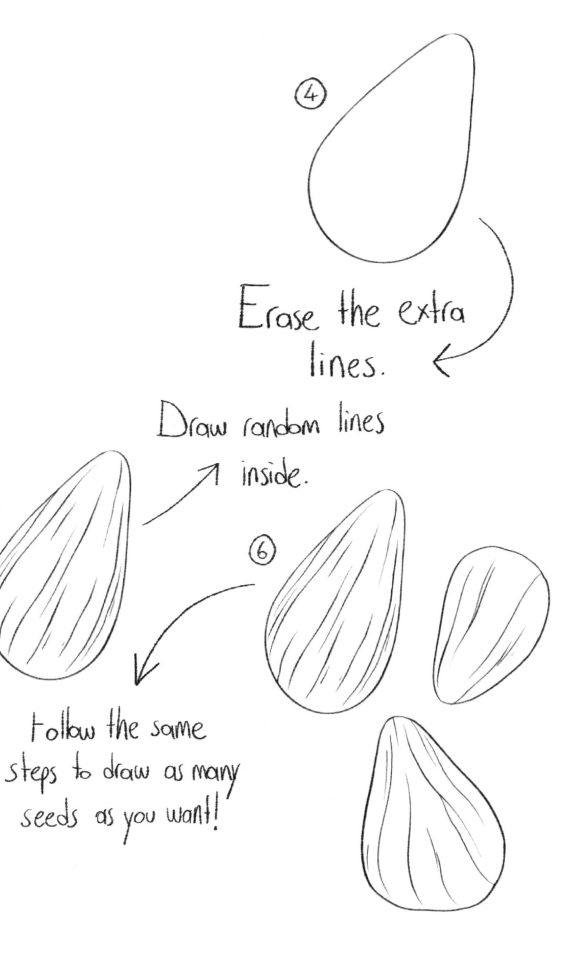

④

Erase the extra
lines.

Draw random lines
inside.

⑤

⑥

Follow the same
steps to draw as many
seeds as you want!

SPROUT

Draw a random
shape.

①

Keep drawing more
random shapes.

②

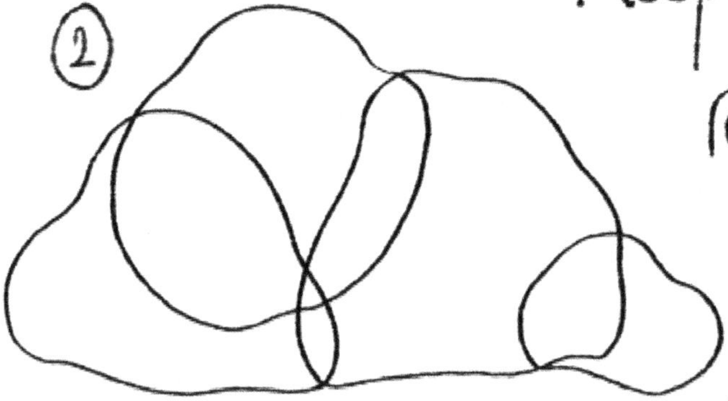

Now erase the
extra lines.

③

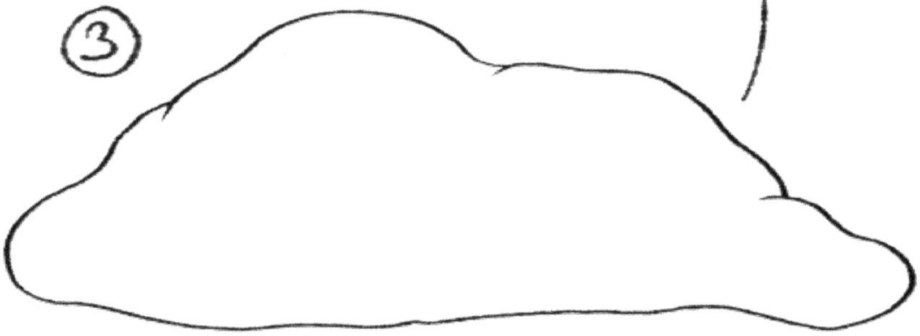

Draw a line on top of the main shape.

Let's draw the leaves.

④

⑤

Draw a straight line inside each leaf.

⑥

NEST

Start with a rounded rectangle.

①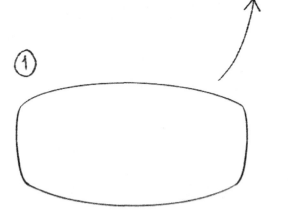

Add random curved lines
inside the main shape.

②

③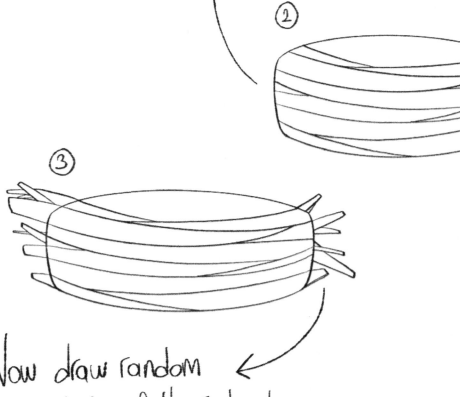

Now draw random
shapes outside of the rectangle.

Erase the extra lines.

④

⑤ Let's draw the eggs.

Final touches and we are done!

⑥

DUCKLING

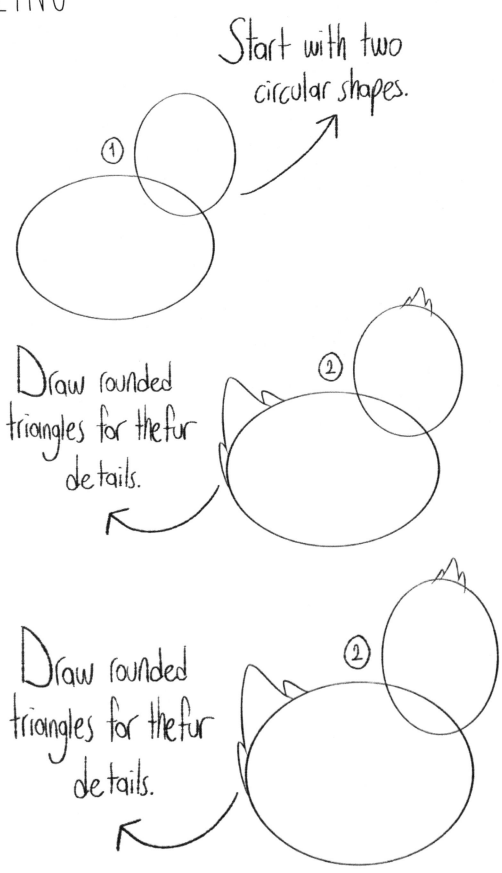

Start with two circular shapes.

Draw rounded triangles for the fur details.

Draw rounded triangles for the fur details.

④

Now draw the beak.

Erase the extra lines.

⑤

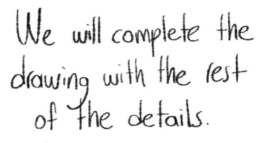

We will complete the drawing with the rest of the details.

⑥

BEE

Start with an ellipse.

①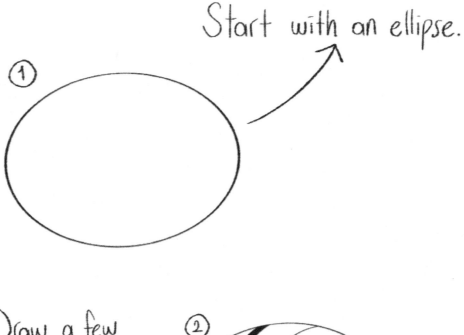

Draw a few curved lines on top of the ellipse.

②

Draw two circular shapes on top of the main shape.

③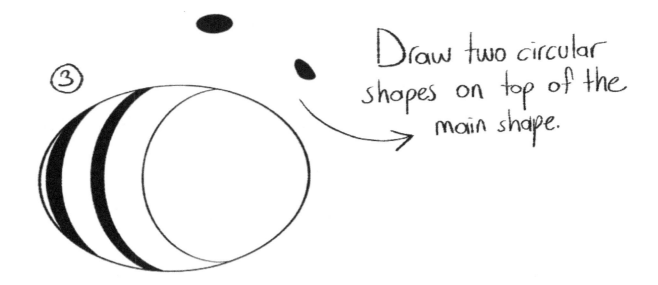

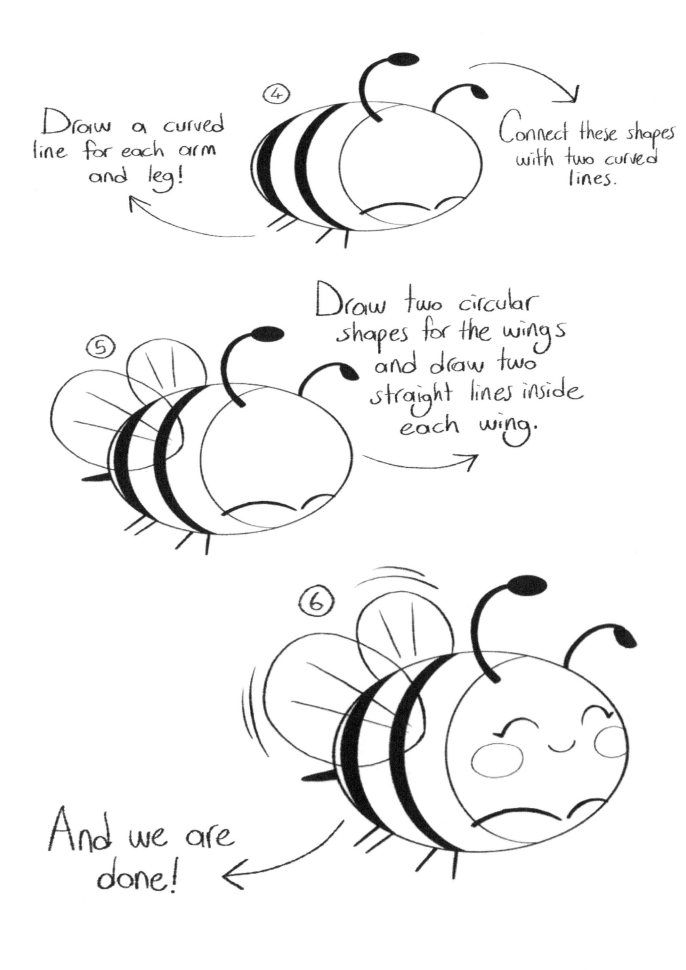

Draw a curved line for each arm and leg!

④

Connect these shapes with two curved lines.

⑤

Draw two circular shapes for the wings and draw two straight lines inside each wing.

⑥

And we are done!

PUDDLE

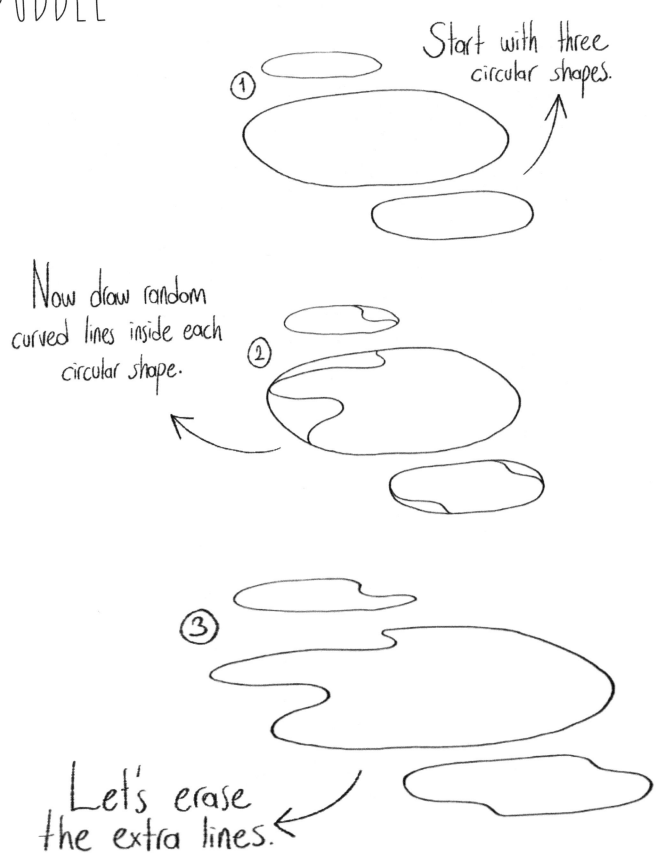

Start with three circular shapes.

①

Now draw random curved lines inside each circular shape.

②

③

Let's erase the extra lines.

Now draw
small circular shapes.

④

Draw random lines inside
each circular shape.

⑤

Now draw lots of short
lines for the rain.

⑥

FLOWER

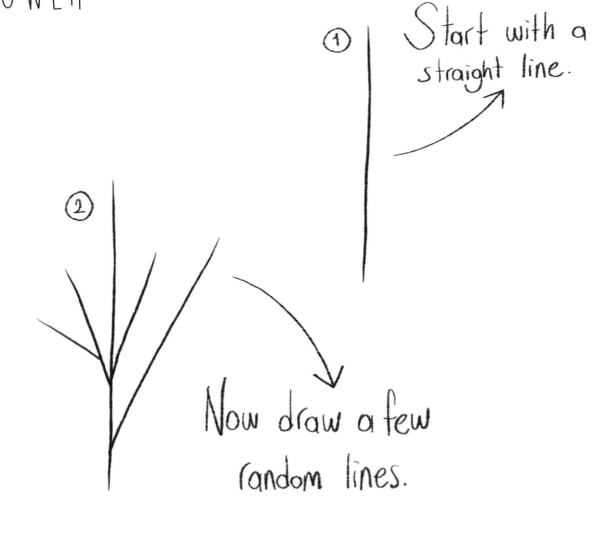

① Start with a straight line.

② Now draw a few random lines.

③ Draw lots of short straight lines.

④

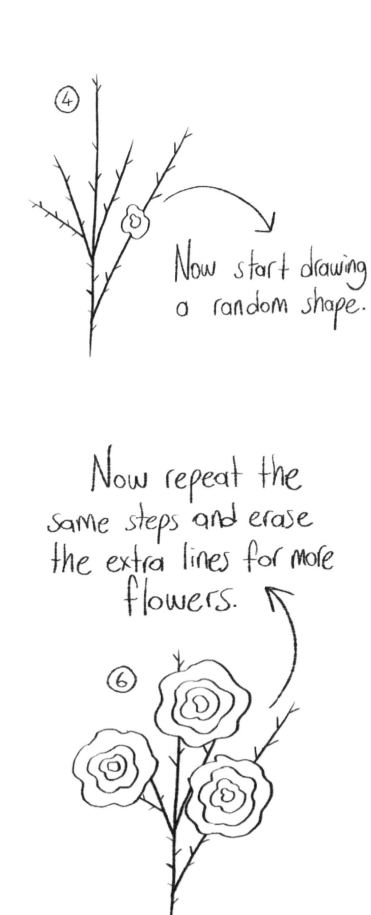

Now start drawing a random shape.

Keep going!

⑤

Now repeat the same steps and erase the extra lines for more flowers.

⑥

UMBRELLA

Draw a curved line.

①

Let's draw more curved lines to form a basic shape of the umbrella.

②

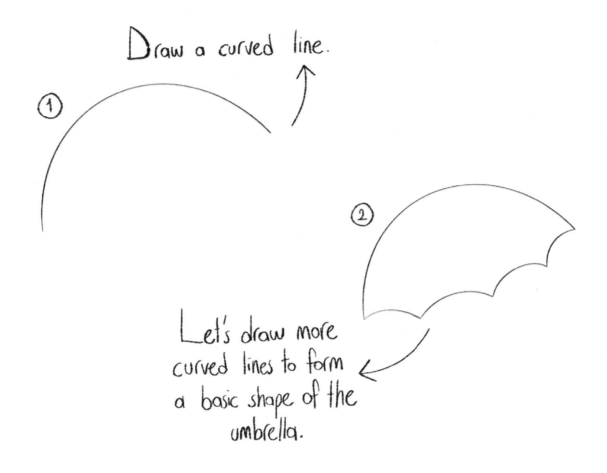

③

Now start drawing a curved line from each corner to the top.

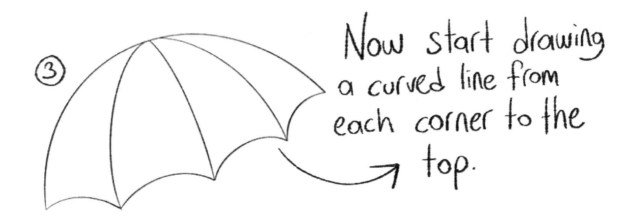

④ Think this shape as a big J.

⑤ Fill it black.

Let's draw circular shapes and we are done!

⑥

MUSHROOM

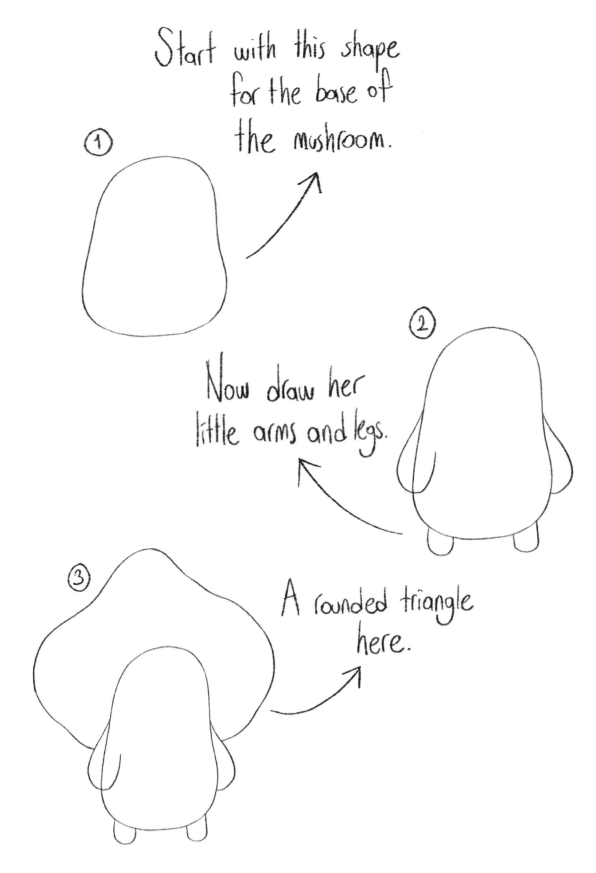

Start with this shape for the base of the mushroom.

①

Now draw her little arms and legs.

②

③

A rounded triangle here.

④

Now draw a circular shape and add lots of curved lines.

⑤

Draw lots of circular shapes and fill it black.

⑥

Let's draw a cute face for our little mushroom and we are done!

KITE

Draw a square.

①

② Now draw two straight lines.

③ Fill these areas black.

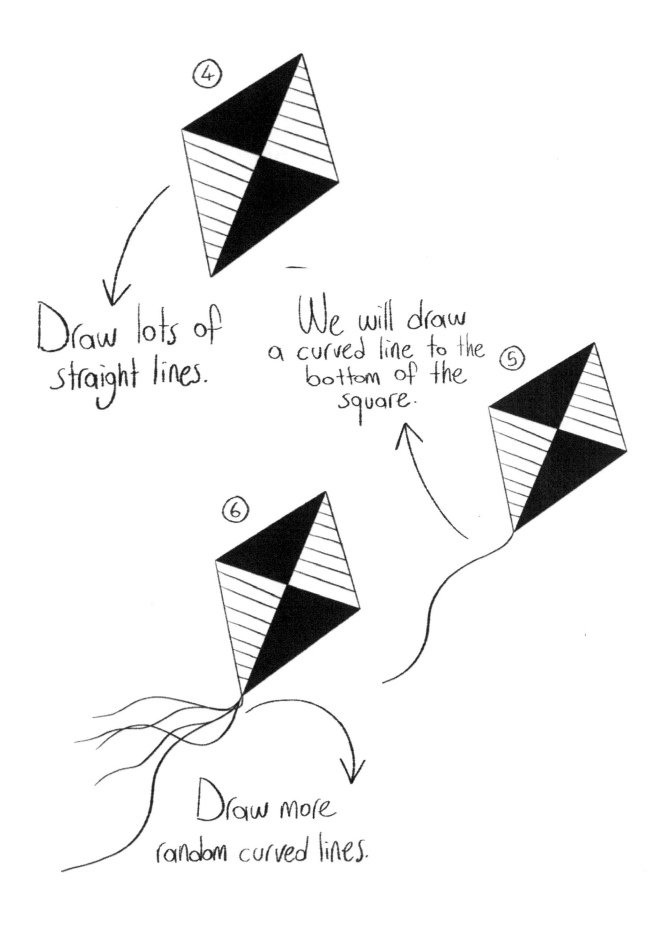

④

Draw lots of
straight lines.

We will draw
a curved line to the
bottom of the
square.

⑤

⑥

Draw more
random curved lines.

SUN

① Draw a circular shape.

Draw short ellipse shapes around the circle.

②

③ Now draw lots of long ellipses.

④ Let's draw the eyes!

⑤ Two more circular shapes for the blush

⑥ Finally draw the mouth and we are done!

CLOUD

① Start with a circular shape.

② Draw two small circular shapes around the first shape.

③ Let's keep drawing more circular shapes.

Let's keep drawing
more circular shapes.

④

Now erase extra lines and
we have a fluffy
shape!

⑤

You can draw a face
to our fluffy friend
or not! It's up to you.

⑥

RAIN

① Start with a circle.

② Now draw a small circle here.

③ Connect the circles with two curved lines.

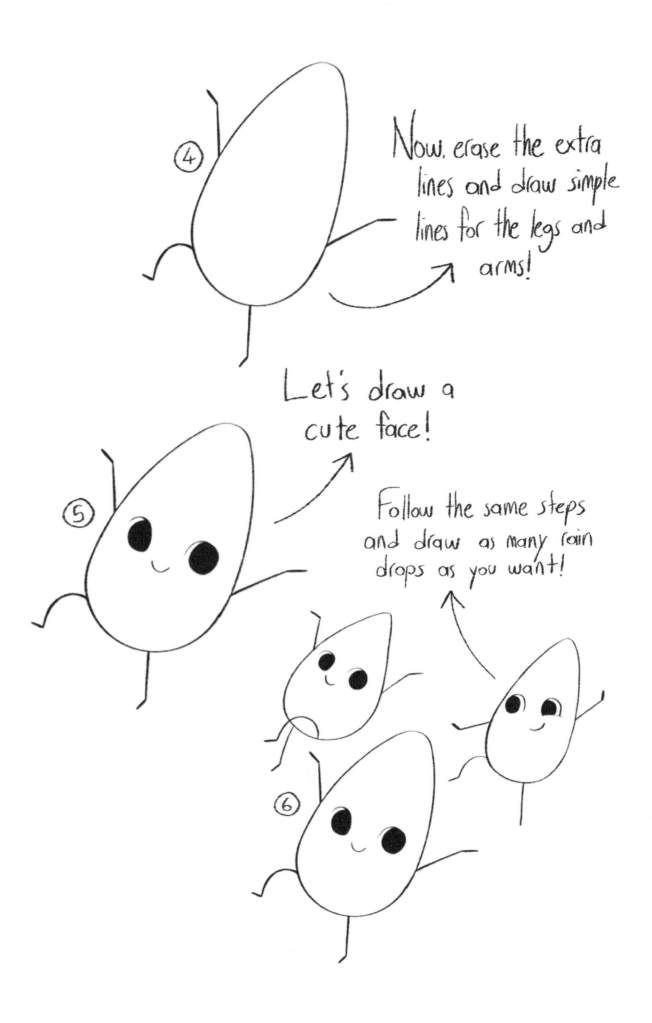

④ Now, erase the extra lines and draw simple lines for the legs and arms!

Let's draw a cute face!

⑤

Follow the same steps and draw as many rain drops as you want!

⑥

LOOKING FOR MORE?
YOU CAN GET FREE LESSONS
AND DISCOUNTED BOOKS FROM
WWW.JOSEPHSTEVENSON.COM

FROG

Start with an ellipse.

①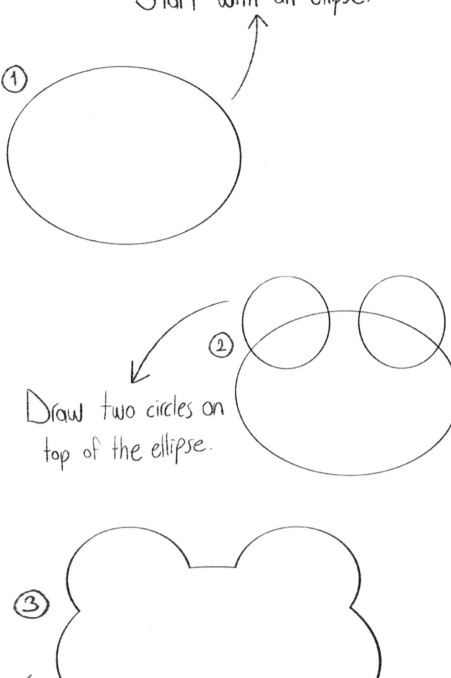

② Draw two circles on top of the ellipse.

③ Erase the extra lines.

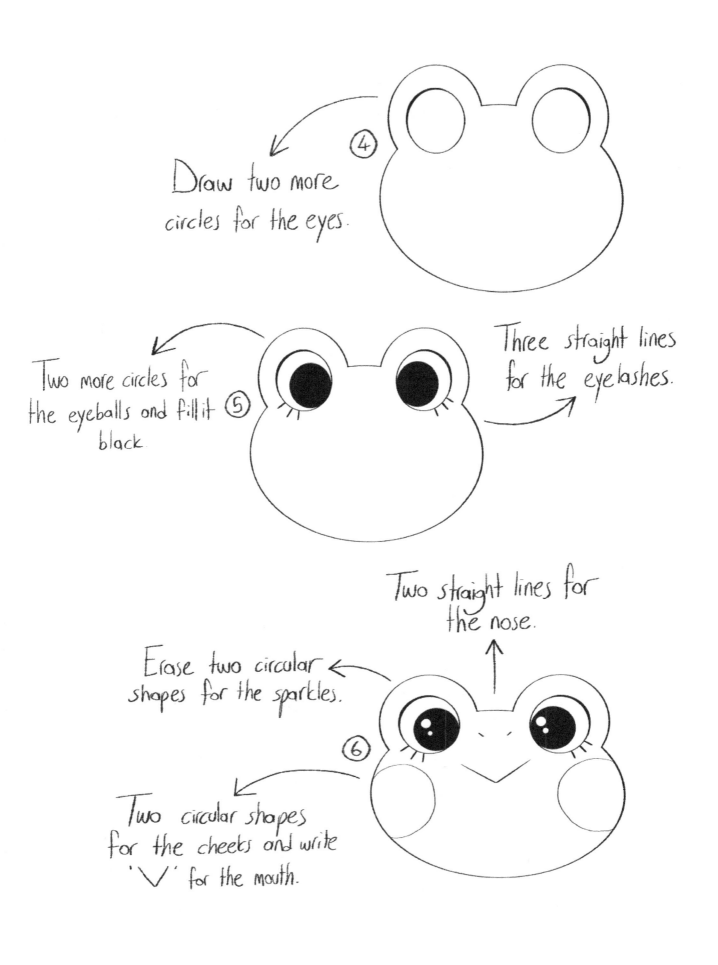

④ Draw two more circles for the eyes.

⑤ Two more circles for the eyeballs and fill it black.

Three straight lines for the eyelashes.

Two straight lines for the nose.

Erase two circular shapes for the sparkles.

⑥ Two circular shapes for the cheeks and write 'V' for the mouth.

SNAIL

Draw this shape for the body of the snail.

①

Now draw two circles for the eyes.

②

Connect these shapes with two straight lines.

③

Draw two circles for the eyeballs, two straight lines for the eyelashes and a curved line for the mouth.

④

Now draw a circular shape for the shell.

⑤

We are done!

⑥

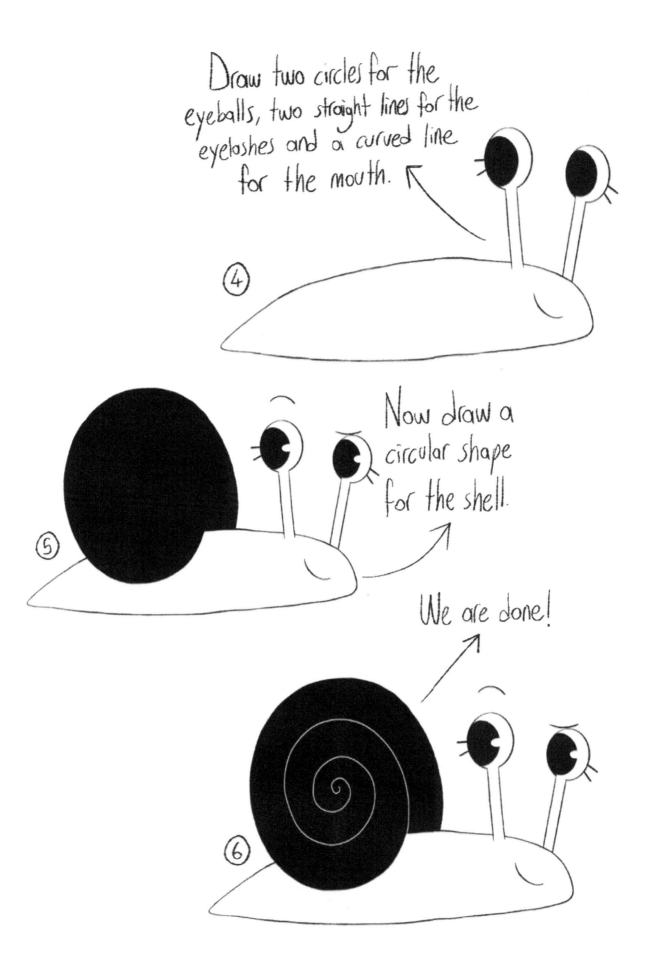

ROBIN

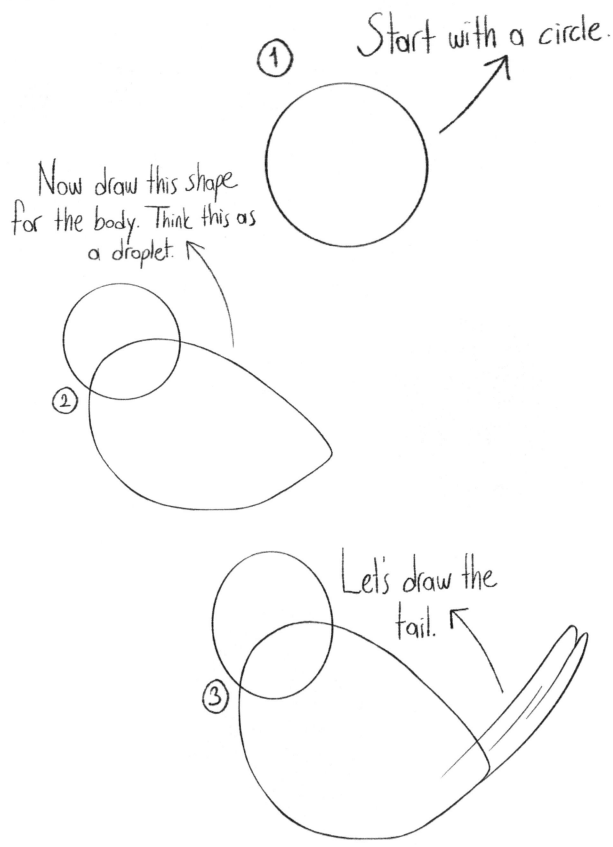

① Start with a circle.

Now draw this shape for the body. Think this as a droplet. ②

Let's draw the tail. ③

Think this shape as 'M'.

Now draw a round triangle for the wing.

④

Erase the extra lines.

⑤

Now, draw the remaining details of the Robin and we are done!

⑥

EASTER CUPCAKE

Draw this rectangle for the base of the cupcake.

①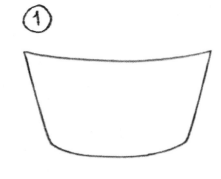

Fill this shape with straight lines.

②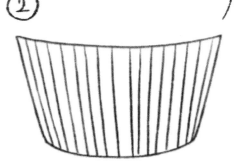

We will add this shape on top.

③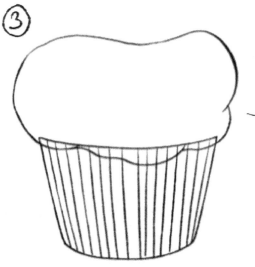

④

Add a few drops to this shape.

Draw lots of rectangles with rounded rectangles.

⑤

⑥

I drew three candy eggs but you can draw as many as you like!

EASTER CAKE

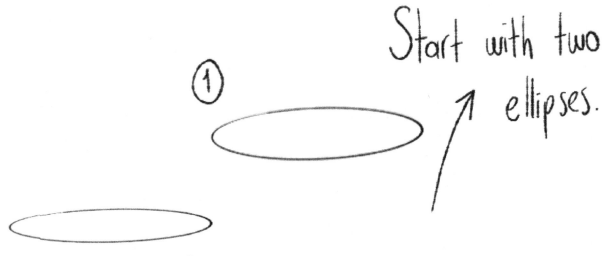

① Start with two ellipses.

Connect these shapes with two straight lines.

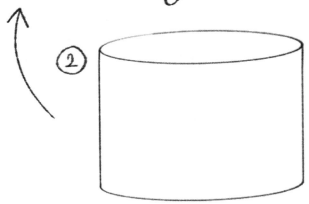

②

③ Lets draw a rose.

Add a few flowers
and erase the extra lines.

④

Draw a curved shape
on top of the cake.

⑤

Finally, we will draw
two curved lines for bunny
ears and draw random lines
on top.

⑥

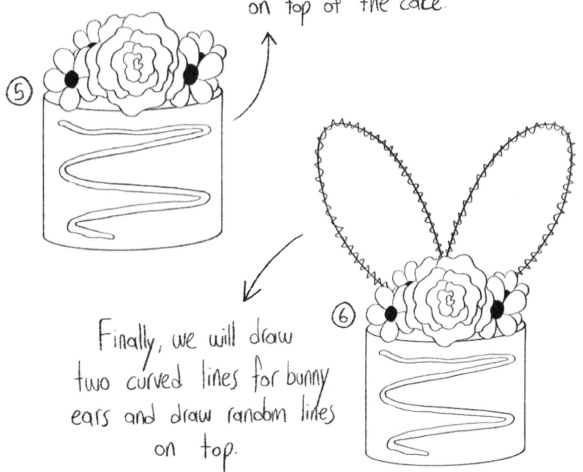

BAGELS

①

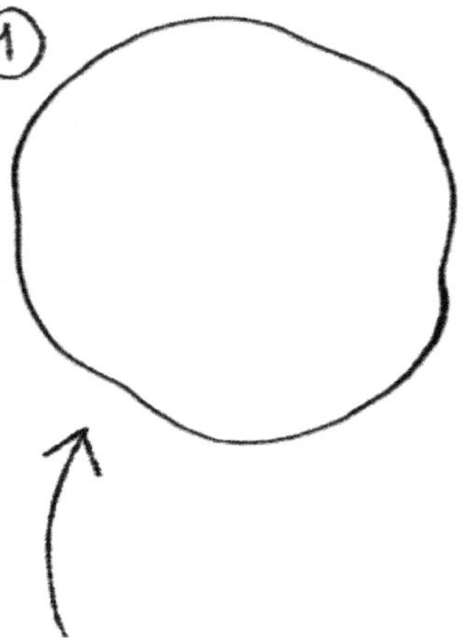

Start with
a circular
shape.

②

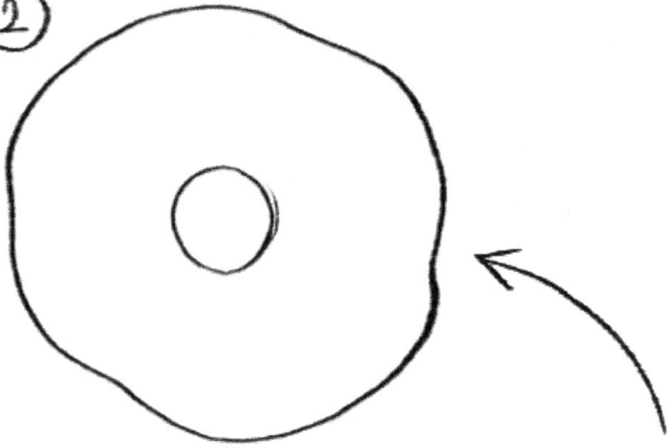

Draw a circle
here.

③

Lets draw another
circular shape.

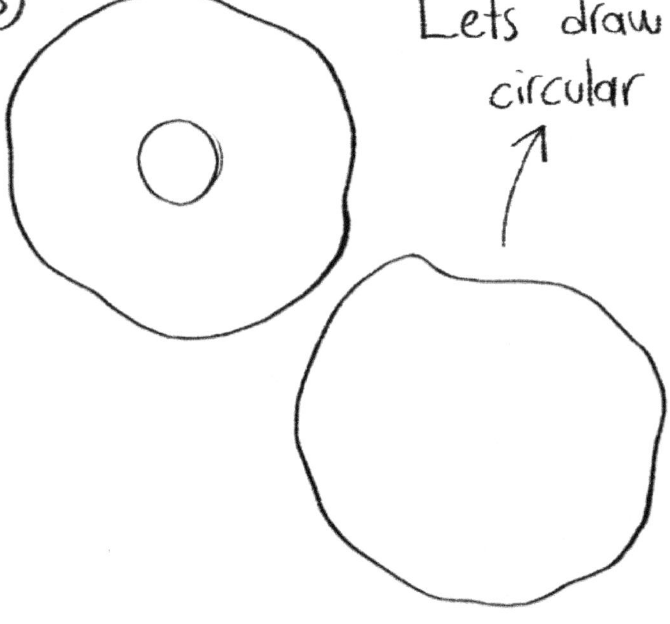

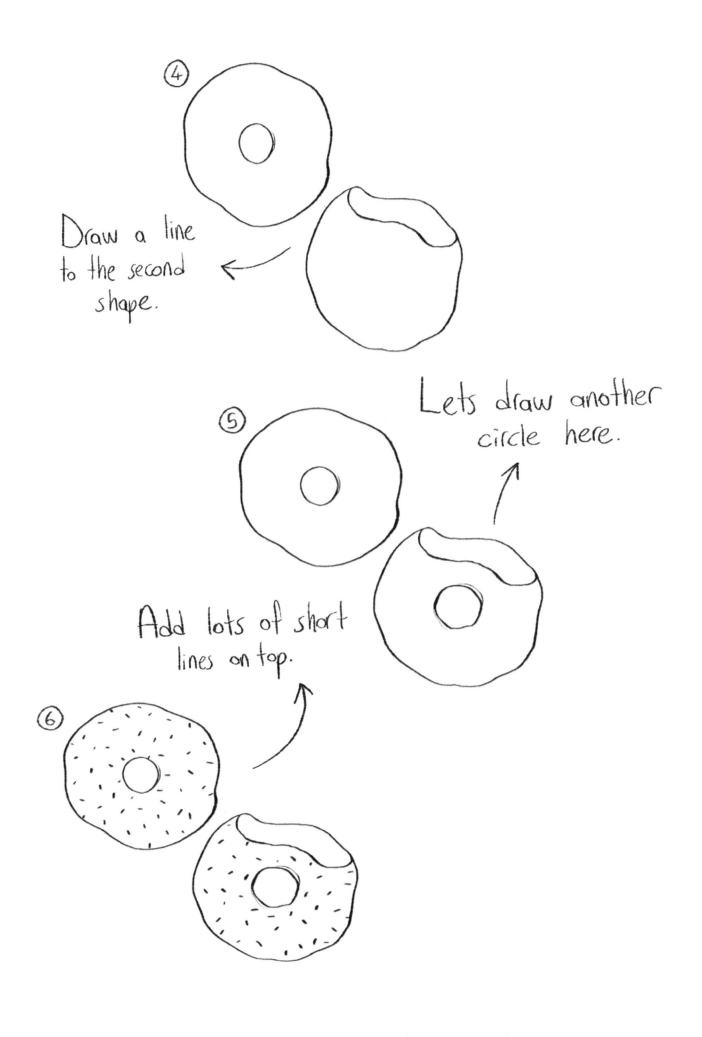

④

Draw a line to the second shape.

⑤

Lets draw another circle here.

Add lots of short lines on top.

⑥

CHOCOLATE EGG

① Start with an ellipse.

② Draw another ellipse.

③ Another ellipse inside the first egg.

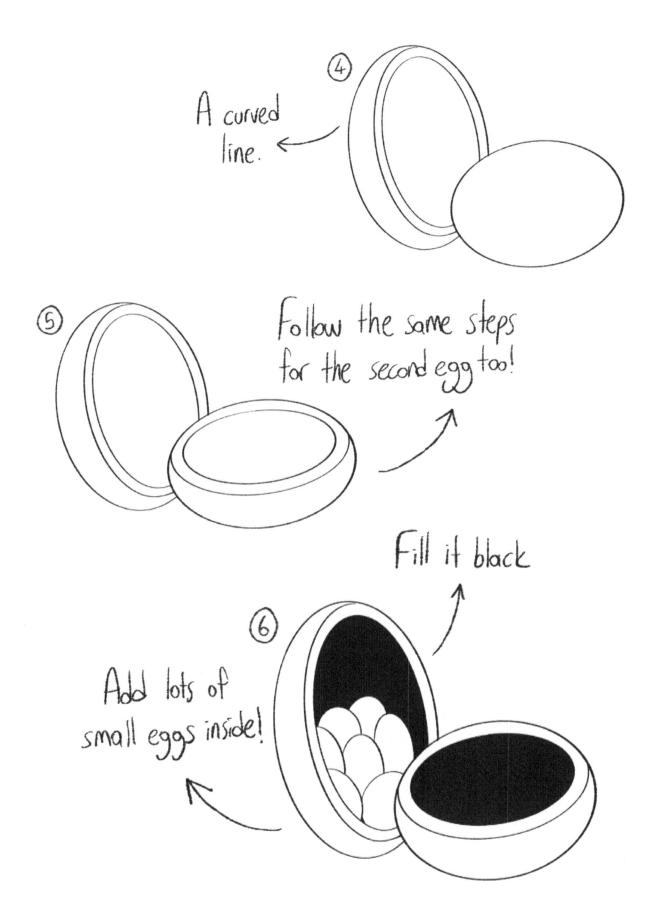

④ A curved line.

⑤ Follow the same steps for the second egg too!

⑥ Fill it black

Add lots of small eggs inside!

HATCH

①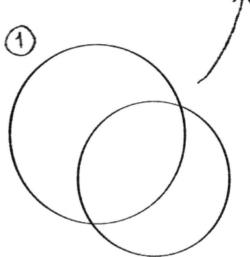

Connect two circles
with two curved
lines.

②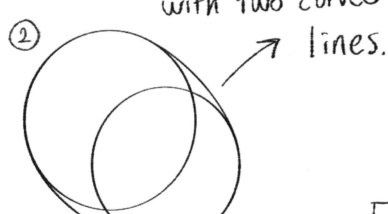

Erase the extra lines
inside.

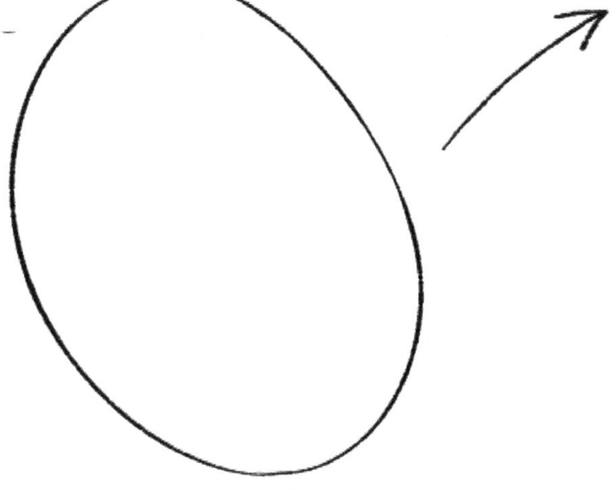

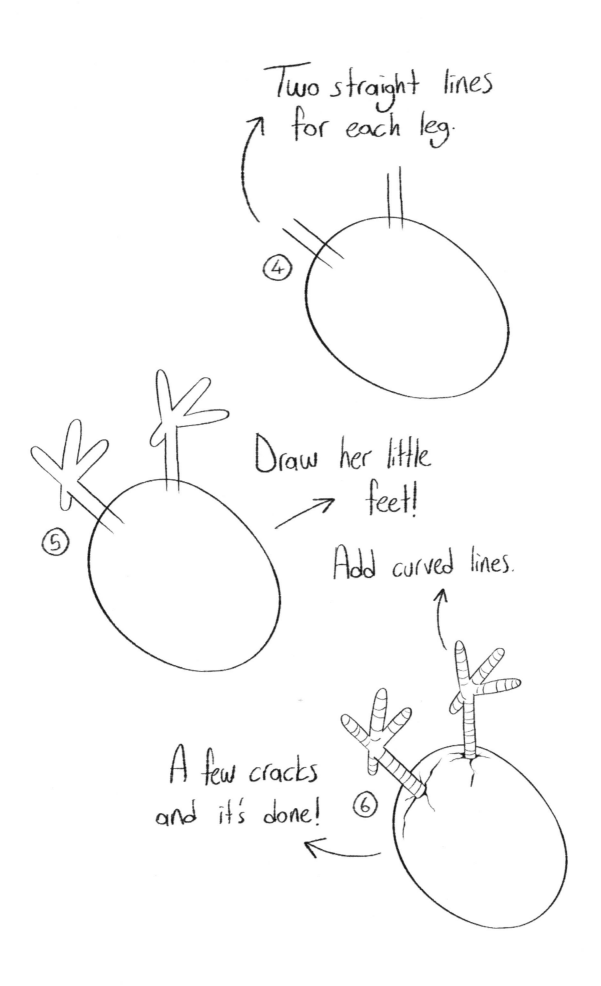

Two straight lines for each leg.

④

Draw her little feet!

⑤

Add curved lines.

A few cracks and it's done!

⑥

PEEPS

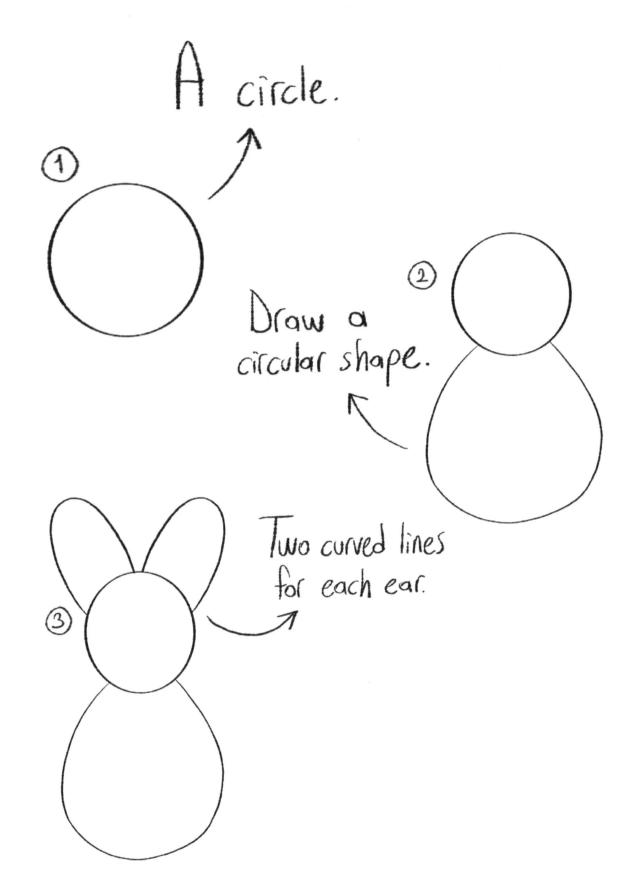

A circle.

①

Draw a
circular shape.

②

Two curved lines
for each ear.

③

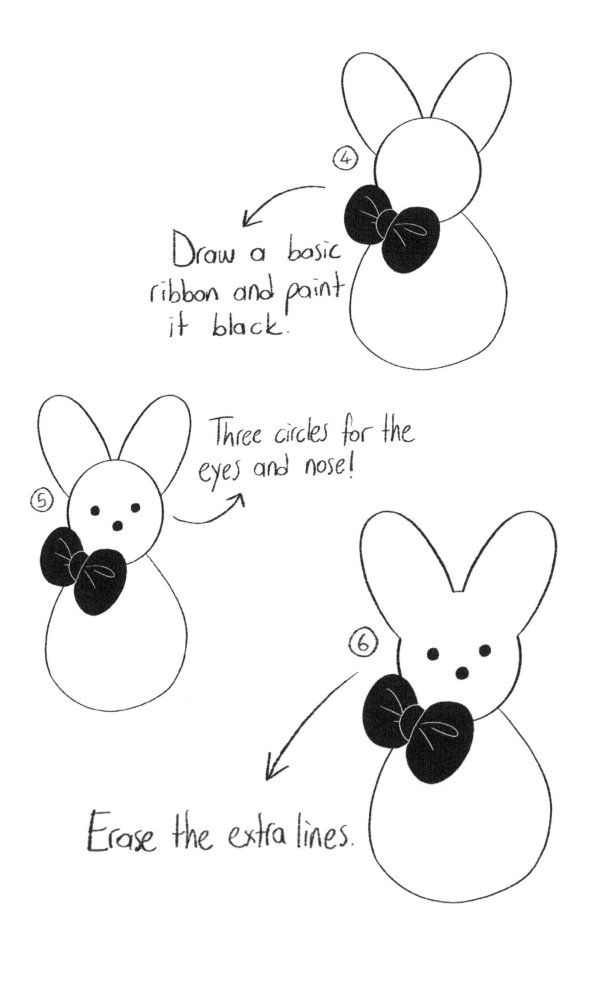

④ Draw a basic ribbon and paint it black.

⑤ Three circles for the eyes and nose!

⑥ Erase the extra lines.

PAINT

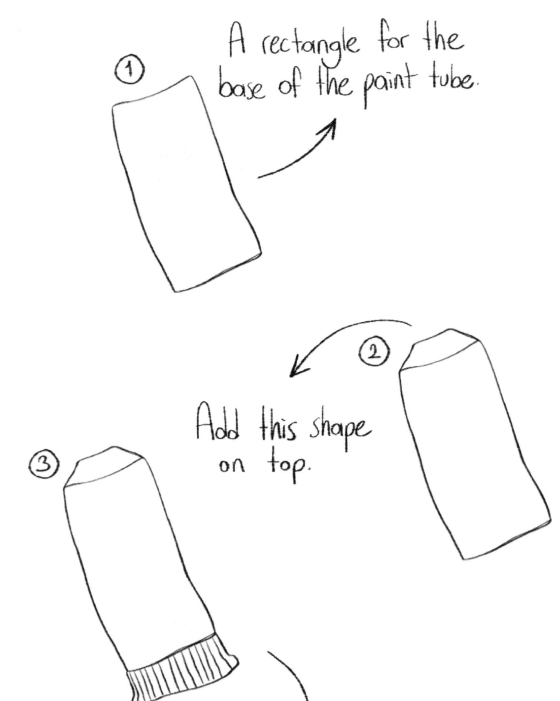

① A rectangle for the base of the paint tube.

② Add this shape on top.

③ Draw another rectangle and draw straight lines inside.

Another rectangle and straight lines!

④

Draw this shape!

⑤

⑥

You can write anything you want here!

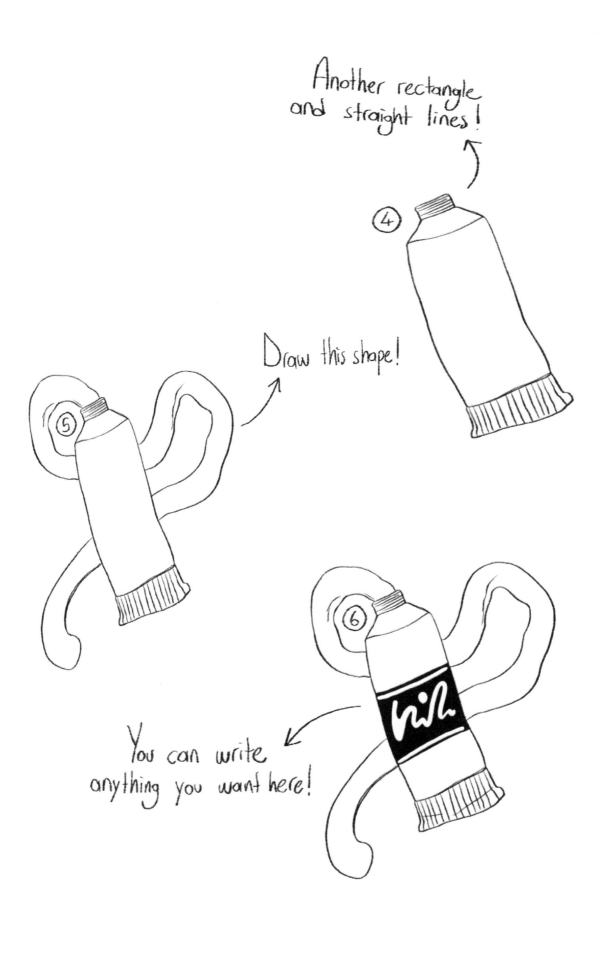

BRUSH

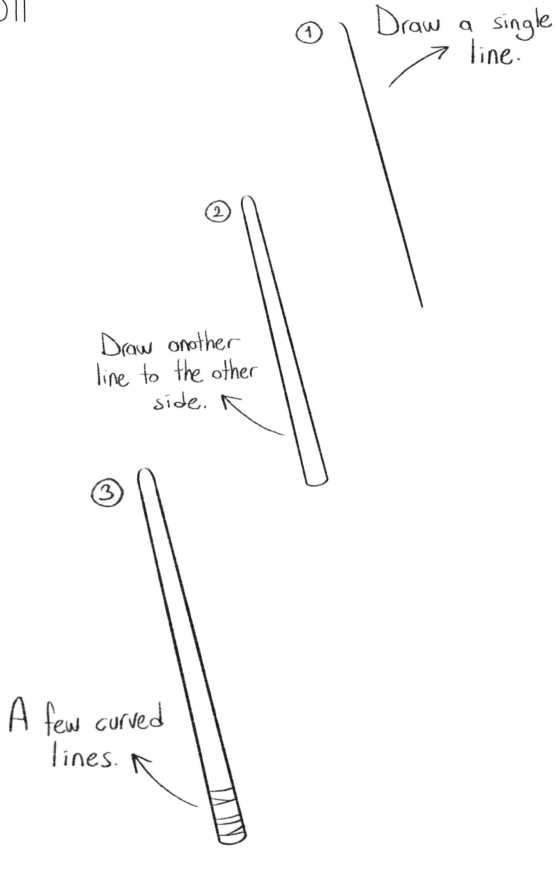

① Draw a single line.

② Draw another line to the other side.

③ A few curved lines.

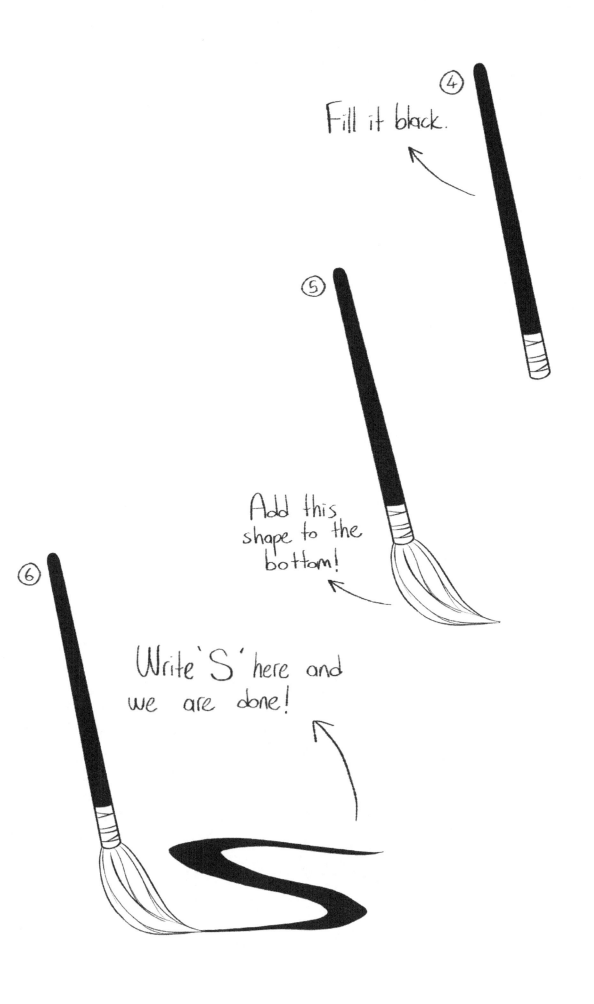

CANDY EGGS

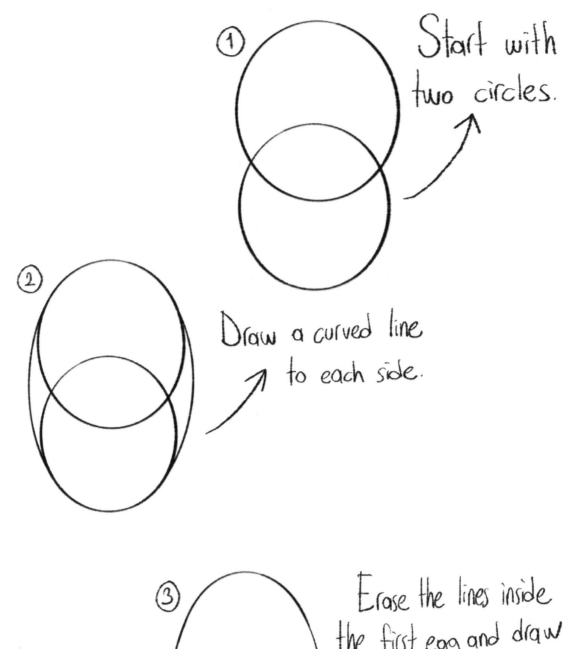

① Start with two circles.

② Draw a curved line to each side.

③ Erase the lines inside the first egg and draw another ellipse for the second egg.

④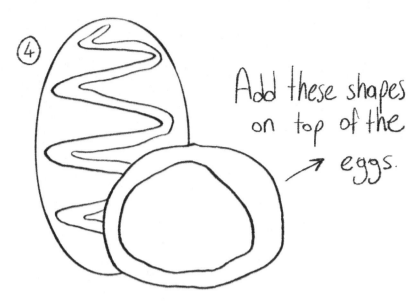

Add these shapes on top of the eggs.

Fill it black.

⑤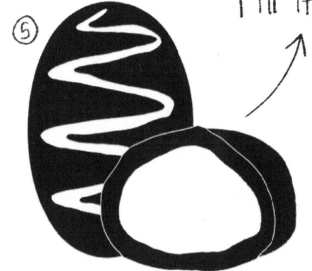

Erase random shapes for the sprinkles.

⑥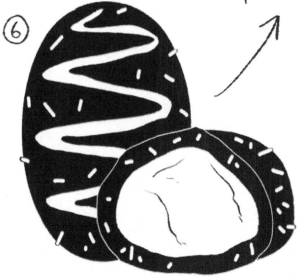

LAMB

① Start with a circle for the base of the head.

② Draw this shape for the mouth.

③ Lets add a fluffy hair on top!

④ Two cute ears!

⑤ Erase the extra lines!

Two circular shapes for the eyes.

⑥ Finish the drawing with the remaining details!

CHOCOLATE

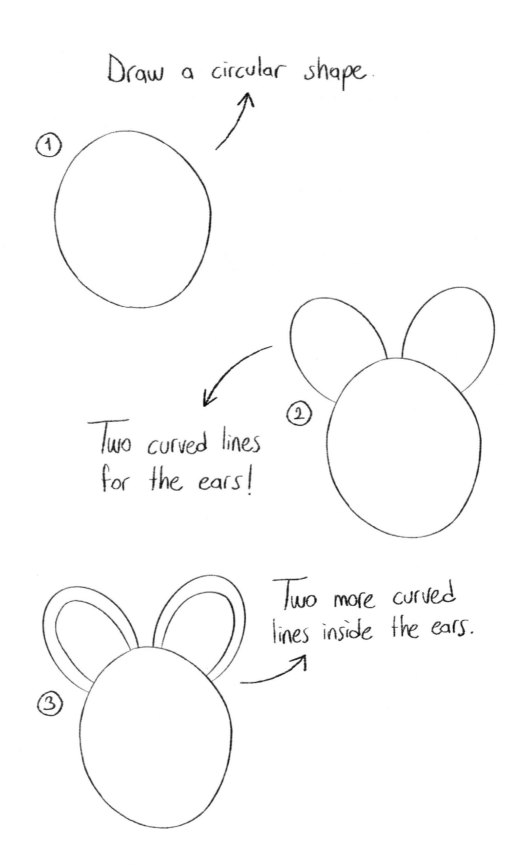

Draw a circular shape.

①

Two curved lines for the ears!

②

Two more curved lines inside the ears.

③

Two rounded rectangles. ④

Erase the extra lines.

⑤

We will complete the drawing with a cute face. ⑥

BUNNY EARS

A curved line.

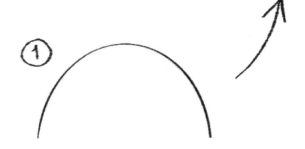

①

Another curved line on top.

②

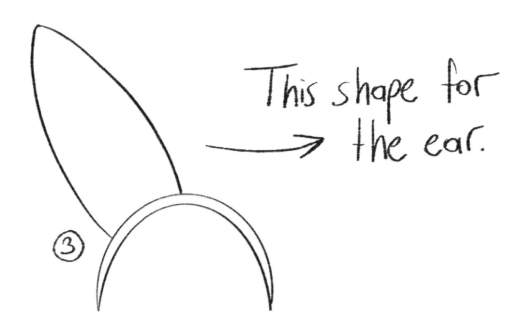

This shape for the ear.

③

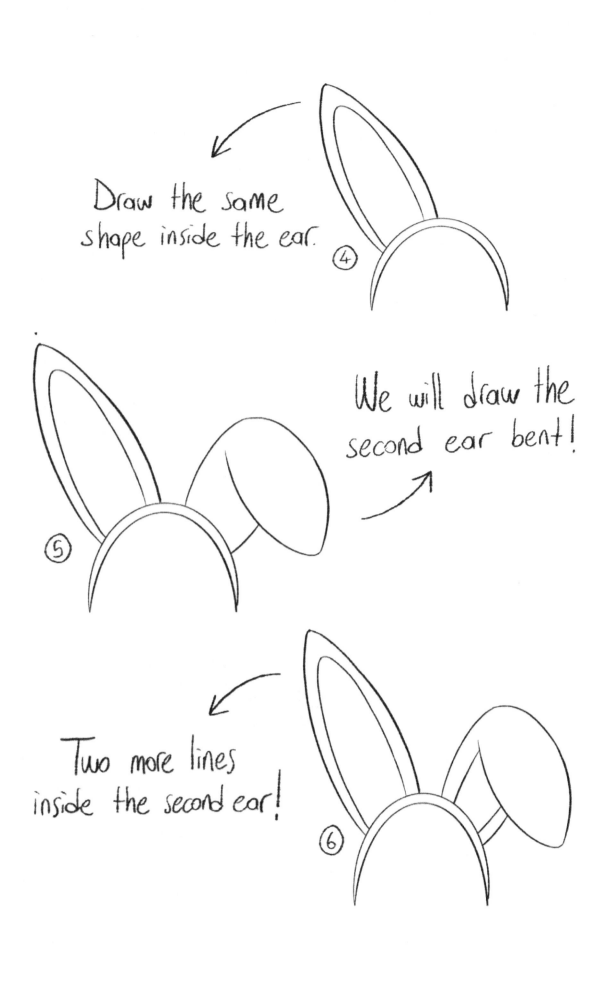

Draw the same
shape inside the ear.

④

We will draw the
second ear bent!

⑤

Two more lines
inside the second ear!

⑥

BOUQUET

Start with two triangle shapes.

①

Think these as combined ellipses.

②

Put some random lines on the shapes.

③

Draw a tiny random shape.

④ Keep adding random shapes and here is the first flower!

⑤ Repeat the same steps and draw as many flowers as you like!

Finish the drawing with various shapes of circles.

⑥

CARROT

Draw an ellipse.

Draw a curved line below and form the base of the carrot.

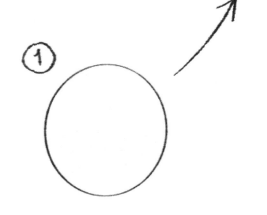

①

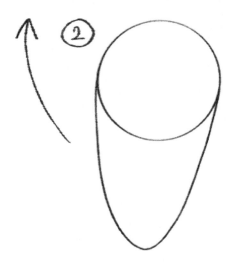

②

③

Add these shapes and fill it black.

Erase the lines inside the carrot.

④ Draw random lines
on top of the carrot.

⑤ Draw a cute face
for the carrot!

⑥ Complete the
drawing with the
final details!

EASTER BONNET

Start with an ellipse.

①

Draw lots of flowers around the circle.

②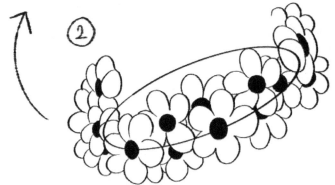

Start with sharp triangle shapes.

③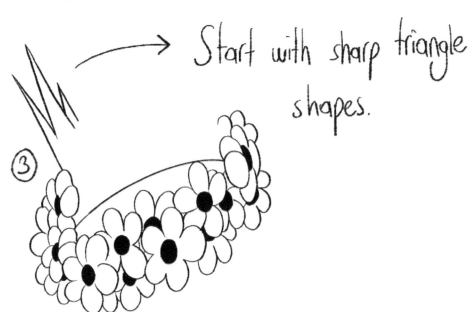

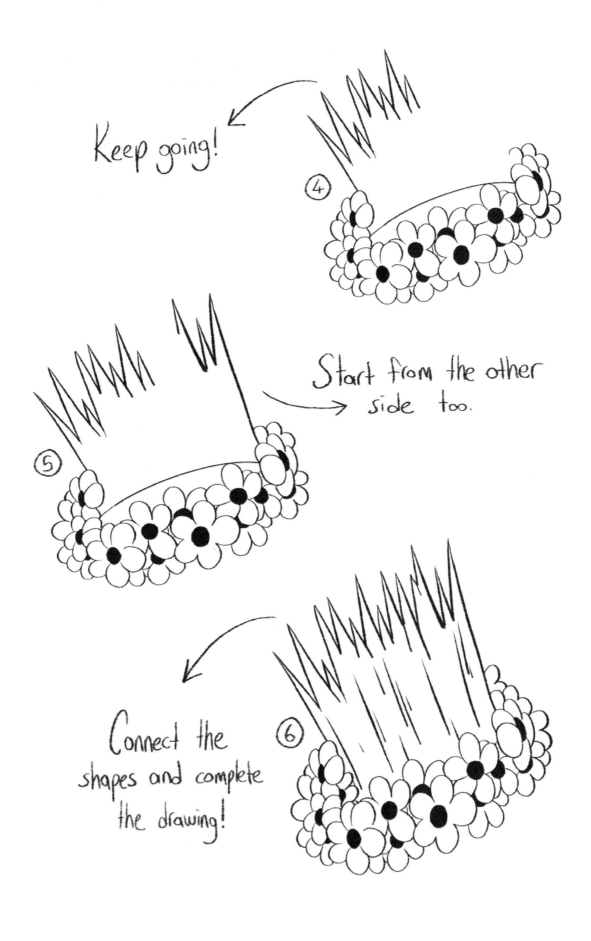

Keep going!

④

Start from the other
side too.

⑤

Connect the
shapes and complete
the drawing!

⑥

JELLY BEANS

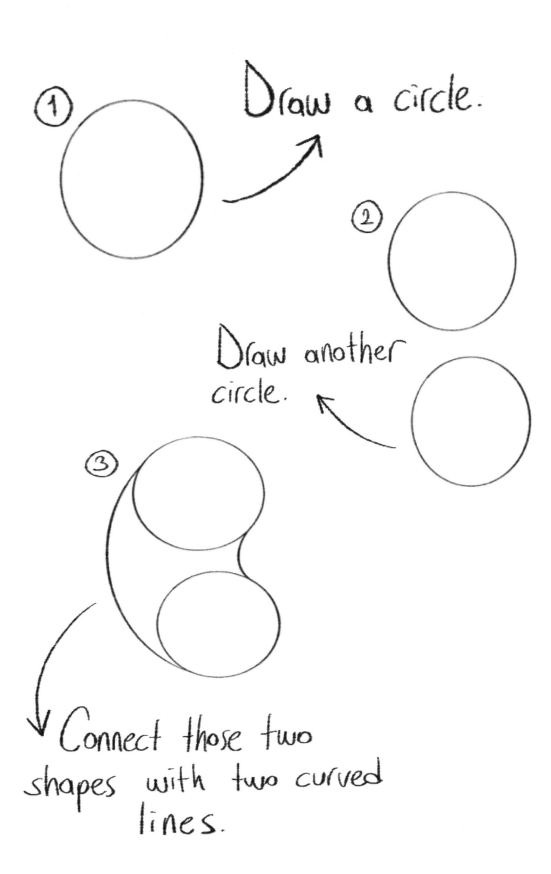

① Draw a circle.

② Draw another circle.

③ Connect those two shapes with two curved lines.

Erase the extra lines
and draw a cute face.

Follow the same steps
and draw another jelly
bean.

Draw another
face and we are
done!

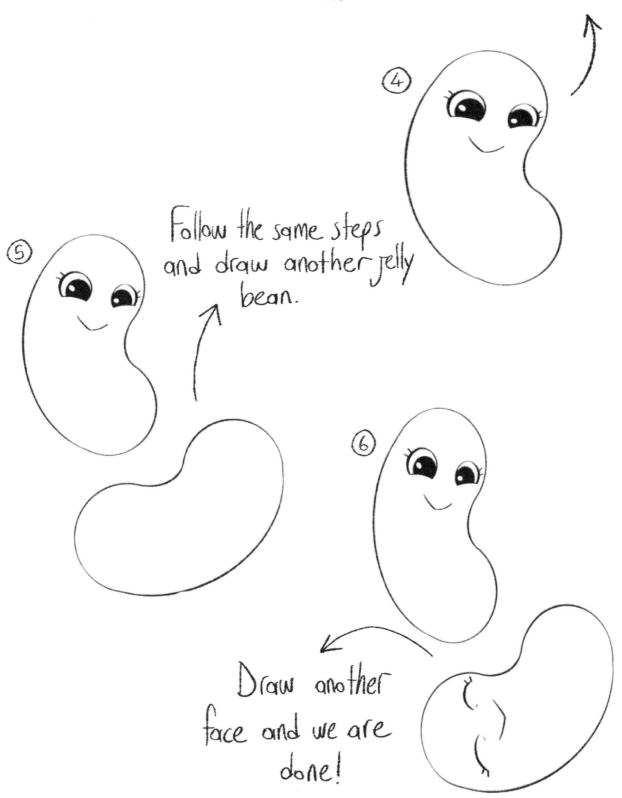

GRASS

① Start with a triangle shape.

② Two more triangles.

③ I know... More triangles!

④ Lets add more grass beneath.

⑤ Lets add more grass beneath.

⑥ You can keep going with these shapes!

LILY

① Start with a
curved line.

② Draw these
leaf shapes.

③ Draw random lines
and add circles on top.

④

Think these shapes as wiggly triangles.

⑤

Keep going!

We are done!

⑥

DON'T FORGET TO FOLLOW
JOSEPH ON SOCIAL MEDIA AND
SIGN UP FOR THE

"NEW BOOK NEWSLETTER"

ON:

WWW.JOSEPHSTEVENSON.COM

Made in the USA
Middletown, DE
25 March 2021